Everything You Need to Know
About the World by Simon Eliot

Everything You Need to Know About the World by Simon Eliot

Thomas Dunne Books
St. Martin's Griffin
New York

≈

Designed and illustrated by Timon Maxey

www.thomasdunnebooks.com
www.stmartins.com

Library of Congress Cataloging-in-Publication Data

Jones, Lloyd, 1955–
  Everything you need to know about the world by Simon
Eliot / Lloyd Jones—1st. St. Martin's Griffin ed.
    p. cm.
  ISBN-13: 978-0-312-35965-2 (alk. paper)
  ISBN-10: 0-312-35965-9 (alk. paper)
  1. Curiosities and wonders—Juvenile literature. 2.
Handbooks, vade mecums, etc.—Juvenile literature. I.
Title.

AG243.J67 2007
013.02—dc22

                                         2007014358

First published in New Zealand in 2004
by the Four Winds Press

First St. Martin's Griffin Edition: July 2007

10 9 8 7 6 5 4 3 2 1

Everything You Need to Know
About the World by Simon Eliot

Everything You Need to Know About the World

By Simon Eliot

Here is the first complete world I
ever saw:

Some spiders build a cobweb
every morning and destroy
it in the evening again.
Fresh cobwebs are nearly
always invisible. You only
see a cobweb because it is
covered with dust.
What I like about spiders
is that they create their
own world.
And this is what I've
done with this book. I've
created my own world. It's
a kind of cobweb of stuff.
A lot of it I found out on
the Web—that other world
wide Web they say is big
enough to hold all the
world's information. The
rest of the info in this
book is a result of my own
genius.

Intestinal stuff

"Garbage in, garbage out."
This is an old saying from
the computer industry. But
it's a saying that applies
just as much to your mind,
body and soul. Eat crap,
feel crap.

On the same subject, a
famous old guy, Socrates,
said: "Other men live to
eat, I eat to live." Think
about it.

But did you know this saying -
"a dog returns to its vomit."
It's from the Bible. "As a dog
returneth to his vomit: so a fool
returneth to his folly."

The reason for vomiting or puking or
throwing up, however you want to say
it, is to get something you don't
want out of your stomach. There are
lots of causes. Drinking too much.
Eating rat poison. Eating too much.

Give a farm pig enough food and it will keep eating
until its stomach bursts and it dies. That's why when
you eat heaps
of food you get
called "a pig."

Check out the <u>vomitorium</u> website *latin meaning to exit*
where people write in and share
vomiting stories. Apparently
fossilized vomit belonging to a
large marine reptile has been found
and is 160 million years old.

Slang for vomit: chuck, chunder,
puke, barf, throw up, Ralph, spew.

Vomit is a combination of hard-to-digest bits of
food and a clear, slimy liquid called gastric mucous,
saliva, hydrochloric acid, and enzymes. Chyme and
bile give vomit that green
color. Vomiting is also
called "a technicolor
yawn."

If you hate
vomiting,
make sure
you wash
your hands
before eating. And if you like
to eat with your hands remember
to say this when they tell you
off: "Fingers were made before
forks."

"First come, first served" is an
old French saying from the 13th
century. Its original meaning was
that those who come to the mill
first may grind their maize first.
Now it's pretty much the story of
fast food sold everywhere.

I need faster food!

7

So why are veggies good for you?

The body needs lots of different food groups to provide the nutrients that make it run smoothly. Think of a car. You don't stuff it with just petroleum. It needs water. It needs oil. If you just stuck petroleum in it and ignored the other things it would soon die a car death.

The body needs different nutrients.

Veggies like carrots and celery are high in vitamins and nutrients. Vitamins and nutrients are to our bodies what oil is to a car.

So what about chocolate? This is soul food. Chocolate also gives you a quick burst of energy. If your parents get tight with the chocolate tell them what Montezuma, Aztec emperor (1480–1520) had to say about hot chocolate: "The divine drink which builds up resistance and fights fatigue. A cup of this precious drink permits a man to walk for a whole day without food."

If that fails, tell them what scientists have found out. Chocolate protects against heart disease and high blood pressure.

If you still have a fight on your hands break chocolate down to its essentials. Tell them it contains important vitamins A, B1, C, D, and E.

Then while you have them stunned but not quite on the floor, tell them you need to eat the stuff for a school project. Ok. We are into last resort territory. Here's the basic gist: chocolate, in its original form, was invented by the Aztecs. Chocolate is made from the cocoa bean found in pods growing from the trunk and lower boughs of the Cacao Tree. Its Latin name *Theobroma cacao* means "food of the gods." So tell them eating chocolate is like a religious studies project. If that fails tell them it's a history project. So you need to know that the first solid chocolate was made in 1847 by Fry & Sons, in Bristol, England. In 1875, the first milk chocolate was made by the Swiss Daniel Peters.

This brings us to the bathroom, crapper, loo, toilet, little girls' room, thunderbox, powder room, privy, potty, whatever. Most people think that the Englishman Thomas Crapper invented the toilet but he didn't. Crapper was in the plumbing business. Crapper made improvements to drains and water closets which is what they used to call toilets or potties. According to historians, WWI soldiers passing through London saw Crapper's name on his shop windows and made the connection. After that it stuck, as in, "I have to go to the crapper." Or, "I have to take a crap."

What's brown and sounds like a bell? Dung!!

9

In Alamo Heights, Texas, a guy called Barney Smith has a toilet seat art museum. He has over 500 toilet seats, which he says are his canvases.

Check out the Virtual Toilet Roll Museum on the Net. It has samples ranging from antique toilet paper and toilet paper from the 19th century to toilet paper with jokes printed on it.

Some important facts:
America is the biggest manufacturer and consumer of toilet paper in the world. But the Americans didn't invent toilet paper.
In 1391, the Chinese Emperor began ordering toilet paper in sheets measuring 2 feet by 3 feet.
In 1857, a New Yorker Joseph Gayetty manufactured the first packaged sheets. These were called "therapeutic paper" and came in packs of 500 for 50 cents.
In 1890, a company called Scott Paper introduced toilet paper on a roll. But the company was too embarrassed to puts its name on the paper.

In 1991, the Americans used toilet paper to
camouflage their tanks in Saudi Arabia during
the Gulf War.
In 1999, Japanese scientists came up with
the paperless toilet. The device washes,
rinses and blow dries the user's bottom.

It is still called carta ingienica "hygienic paper" in Italian

The oldest toilet was found in
Mohenjo Daro in North West India.
It is more than 4,000 years old
and had pipes that ran out into
the streets.

In AD 315, in
ancient Rome, there
were 144 public
toilets. These were
very popular social
places and were
often decorated
with mosaics and
fountains.

The biggest toilet in the world!

The Romans were so much into their toilets they even had a toilet God called Crepitus.

In England the first toilet goes back to 1596 when Queen Elizabeth's godson made her an early version of a potty. This version was to your modern flush toilet what the first kite was to the modern airplane. It was invented by Sir John Harrington. His friends all thought it a joke. Why would you invent a machine for the business when a bucket was as good and at the end you just tossed the slop out the window? Harrington and the Queen were ahead of their time. The Queen and her godson kept using the toilet. Everyone else flung their muck out the window.
It was another 200 years before Sir John's potty was improved on by a man called Alexander Cummings.

In 1777 a man called Samuel Prosser invented the plunger closet. The most famous toilet-maker of them all, Thomas Twyford, made the first all china toilet in 1885.

In fact, toilets have been around longer than that. Over 4,000 years ago there were toilets in the Minoan Palace at Knossus in Crete, which is in the Greek Islands. The Minoans and Romans had restrooms with hot and cold water, and a sewage system that used water to flush away any waste product.

The first public potty was invented by the Romans. The Emperor Vespasian actually made money out of the public potties by collecting the urine and selling it on to the people who dyed cloth.

In Scotland, in the 18th century, vendors walked around the streets selling public potties. They weren't very private. You squatted over a bucket and a guy held a large cloak in front of you.

Still, there were Kings of France who used to go to the toilet while conducting state business. So, I guess, closing the door while you sit on the potty is a recent custom.

Weird when you think about it, but while the body is getting rid of "waste products" those same waste products are great for the soil. Crap, or its official highbrow name feces, is made up of 65 percent water, 15 percent ash, 5 percent nitrogen, and 15 percent of some other stuff that I forget.

Three million Chinese and two million Japanese drink their own urine every day. They also gargle with it or use it as eye or ear drops.

An early German chemist thought he could extract gold from urine. In his cellar he evaporated down 56 pails of urine to make a foul-smelling paste. More evaporation and he produced a tiny blob that glowed in the dark and caught fire. He had discovered phosphorus.

The first wedding
in a public toilet
took place in 1996 in
Taiwan.

Poop in Swahili is kinyesi/vinyesi.

One of history's most famous farters
was a French man by the name of
Joseph Pujol. He was so good at it
that he made his living from giving
public performances.
Joseph discovered his talent at an
early age. His debut at the Moulin
Rouge (a famous nightclub in Paris,
France) in 1892 was a huge success.
Joseph could imitate gunfire and
make mock bugle calls. He would end
his act by farting the opening
bars of the French
National Anthem.

15

In 1980, on Japanese TV a man farted over 3,000 times in a row before a studio audience.

It is definitely uncool times maximum penalty to burp or fart at the dinner table or on a bus or on a train. Even hand farts are uncool because other people around you don't know it's just a hand fart.

What makes farts smell? Hydrogen sulphide gives farts their rotten eggs smell.

Fart in French is "Pet"
"Bah sheet" in Romanian
"Dut" in Vietnamese
"Purrrrd note" in Czech
"Pay dough" in Spanish
"Oh nowla" in Japanese
"Fang pi" in Mandarin

nice pet

= pet

On a related subject, baked beans
were invented by the American
Indians. The first canned baked
beans were made with molasses in
1875. Tomato sauce was added to
the recipe by the Van Camp Packing
Company of Indianapolis in 1891.
Around this time baked beans were
introduced to Britain. Now, more
than 100 years later, Britons eat
twice as much tomato sauce and
beans as Americans.

The first soft drink appeared in the 17th century. It was just lemon juice and honey. Vendors used to carry barrels of it on their backs and hand out cups. Soda is carbonated which means that carbon dioxide is pumped into water to make it fizz. Coca-Cola was invented in 1886 by John Pemberton, a pharmacist.

Fizzy drinks contain a lot of carbon dioxide, which makes you burp or belch. A burp or belch is just gas. When you eat and drink, you swallow air at the same time. The air we breathe contains gases like nitrogen and oxygen. Sometimes when we swallow gases we need to get them out – that's where a really good burp comes into its own.

Famous stuff you can expect to hear a lot about

Klingons are the sworn enemies of humans on **Star Trek**. The Klingon Empire steals whatever it needs from whomever.

nasty types!

Spock is an alien being in *Star Trek*, a Vulcan with green blood. You will know him when you see him. He has pointed ears, and he sleeps with his eyes open.

← awake!

stop bothering me

fable ↓

Aesop was a 6th century BC Greek who wrote fables. He was deformed, and born a slave. After he was freed he did a lot of traveling. Once he was accused of stealing (actually he was set up, so it's written) and he was thrown off a cliff. Somehow he survived that. Some of the stories he went on to write were "The Goose That Laid the Golden Eggs" and "The Lion and the Mouse."

Aladdin is the most famous character of a book called the *Arabian Nights*, set in an ancient Chinese kingdom. Aladdin is always disobeying his father. One day Aladdin is promised riches if he will agree to help a magician. He accepts, and is sent deep into a cave to fetch a lamp. While there he becomes suspicious, and he refuses to hand the lamp over until he is out of the cave. This angers the magician who seals Aladdin in the cave. After two days Aladdin rubs a brass ring and a genie appears and asks him what he would like. He will grant any wish, so Aladdin asks to be set free. When he returns home he finds his mother is starving. Aladdin decides he will sell the lamp. Preparing it for sale he begins polishing it and out comes the genie. The genie promises all that Aladdin desires. Grateful for his good luck, Aladdin becomes a good kid and a reformed character, as they say.

While we are on the A's, you need to know about Amazons. They were a race of heroic women warriors in Greek mythology. They each cut off their right breast so they could better draw their bow and arrow. "A" before a word often means "without." Mazos means breast. Amazon. Got it?

Antaeus, the son of the Greek gods Poseidon and Gaea, was a champion wrestler who lived in a house made from the skulls of his victims.

Dracula is a vampire nobleman who becomes younger by drinking human blood.

Asterix is a comic-strip hero who lived around 50 BC in a small village surrounded by camps of Roman soldiers. A magic drinking potion gives him superhuman strength. His best friend is the giant Obelix who dines on wild boar.

King Arthur was a leader in battle, and one of the Knights of the Round Table. Arthur became king at the age of 15 after he was able to draw a sword that was stuck in a large stone.

Batman is really a guy called Bruce Wayne who vows to fight crime after a thug kills his parents. His body and mind are trained to perfection. But he realizes he will need a disguise, and while he is considering the options he happens to look up and see a bat fly in the window. The idea of batman is born at that very moment.
His enemies are the Joker, the Penguin, Mr. Freeze, Catwoman, and the Scarecrow.
The good guys are Robin, Batwoman, Batgirl, and Bat-Hound.

Animal Farm is a satirical fable written by George Orwell in 1945. Some farm animals start a revolution to run the farm as they want. They are betrayed by their leaders, the Pigs, into a worse state than before. The Pigs' slogan is "All animals are equal, but some animals are more equal than others."

"The Artful Dodger" is a young thief, the pickpocket pupil of master thief, Fagin, in Charles Dickens' novel **Oliver Twist**.

Walt Disney created the character of Mickey Mouse in 1928. He is also famous for Disney Studios, which produced cartoons and films such as *Pinocchio* (1940), *Fantasia* (1940), and *Peter Pan* (1953).

The first full-length animated movie was *Snow White and the Seven Dwarfs*. It was made by Walt Disney in 1937.

Dr. Dolittle is a very unusual veterinarian who can speak 499 different animal languages. He was dreamt up by a soldier called Hugh Lofting during a battle in World War I.

Jack Frost is an elf who discolors leaves in autumn and draws the frost designs over the windowpanes.

Gulliver in **Gulliver's Travels**
(published in 1726) goes to sea
and visits islands inhabited
by little people
(Lilliputians), giants
(Brobdingnag), talking
horses (the Houyhnhnms),
and ghosts (Glubdubdrib).

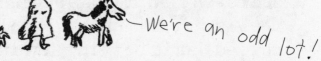

We're an odd lot!

Yahoos are the rough people who
appear in Jonathan Swift's book
Gulliver's Travels.
Not to be confused with the search
engine yahoo.com

"Come into my parlor said the spider to the fly."
That's the first line of "The Spider and the Fly," a
poem written by Mary Howitt (1799–1888). Mary
was born in Coleford, England, and was the first
English translator of Hans Christian Andersen. He
wrote *The Ugly Duckling, The Red Shoes, The
Emperor's New Clothes*, and *The Tinder-Box*.

Andersen was the son of a poor shoemaker and a washerwoman. If that almost sounds like one of his stories, that's because Hans left school at 14 to seek his fortune. He had a go at acting and didn't do very well. He was a tall and skinny guy with a big nose. Hans wrote over 150 fairy tales and these have been translated into more than 100 languages.

Leprechauns are famous fairy shoemakers. Leprechauns stand only two feet tall. Their name comes from Leith Bhrogan which means "the one shoemaker" as leprechauns can only work on one shoe at a time.

 like two suns!

Leviathan was a great sea beast of Biblical legend. His eyes were so big and bright they lit up the entire sea. When he was hungry his hot breath caused the sea to boil. Only the tiny stickleback fish could control Leviathan to stop him from snorting the sea into nothingness.

White Rabbit, the Cheshire Cat, the Mock Turtle, the Queen of Hearts, and the Mad Hatter all appear in *Alice in Wonderland* (written in 1865 by Lewis Carroll). Alice is a small girl who falls down a well into a strange country. She discovers she can become extremely tall or extremely short by nibbling the alternate sides of a special mushroom.

The Little Prince is the story of a boy who travels the world on a search for the roots of human emotion. **The Little Prince** was written by Antoine de Saint-Exupéry who was a French pilot during World War II. The Little Prince lives on an asteroid called B-612.

Popeye is a cartoon character, a muscle-bound sailor who makes his living from boxing and treasure-hunting. He eats a lot of spinach which gives him his strength.

Bart Simpson is a 10-year-old on **The Simpsons**. Bart isn't the smartest guy on the block but he's got a big heart. Bart goes to Springfield Elementary where he gets F in all subjects. **The Simpsons** was the longest running TV animated show—Bart and Homer ran for 300 episodes.

Guiding Light is a TV soap that your parents and grandparents might get excited about. The program first aired in 1952 and will last to Armageddon.

Armageddon sick of it!

Armageddon is the predicted time in the future when the world will end.

Armageddon sick of Armageddon!

"And there were
voices, and thunders,
and lightnings; and
there was a great
earthquake, such
as was not since
men were upon the
earth, so mighty
an earthquake, and so great."
"Book of Revelation," chapter 16,
verse 18, for a description of
Armageddon.

A "couch potato" is someone who sits
through *Guiding Light* and the rest
of the night's programs plus all the
ads without moving his or her butt.

Peter Pan is the kid in J. M.
Barrie's book by the same name.
Peter Pan never grows up. In **Peter
Pan**, Tinkerbell sprinkles fairy
dust on you and all you have to
do is to have a happy thought.
My wish would be to fly. But
humans can't—we are too
heavy and we have no wings.
Birds can fly because they
have lightweight skeletons and
their bones are semi-
hollow like honeycomb
so they can basically
just float in the air
anyway. Their wings
are curved so they
can catch the air and
their feathers catch
the breeze when they
flap.

Achilles is the hero of the *Iliad,* the long poem written by the Greek poet Homer. Achilles took part in the Trojan War on the side of the Greeks and slew the Trojan hero Hector. Achilles had been dipped in the river Styx by his mother, which gave him total immortality and protection except in his heel by which she held him. He was killed by being shot in the heel by an arrow fired by Paris, Hector's younger brother.

The phrase "Achilles' heel" is used to describe the vulnerable part in a person's character.

You need to know about Homer, though not much is actually known about him. No one knows who his parents were. He was a blind poet living around the Ionian Sea. Homer wrote the famous epic stories of the *Iliad* and the *Odyssey*.

"Odyssey" is another word handed us by the Greeks. It means a huge journey as in "Man, we had to wait for the tow truck, walk to the garage, camp for three days before the new car parts arrived—what an odyssey!"

The Flying Carpet appears in stories from the Middle East. The carpet carries its passengers to worlds of the imagination. The story is said to have been inspired by the lazy drifting of clouds.

SOME FAMOUS JOURNEYS & ADVENTURES

Birds that fly south for the winter chalk up huge distances. An Arctic tern found dead on Stewart Island, New Zealand, had flown 15,534 miles from Sweden. The Swedish Museum of Natural History was able to confirm that it was the farthest ever recorded migration of a tagged bird from Sweden. Researchers believe the bird flew south along Africa's west coast, passed South Africa and then turned east across the Indian Ocean.

Arctic terns spend a whole summer in the Arctic, fly south to spend the next summer in the Antarctic. In fact they spend their whole lives in daylight except while migrating.

Some tiny hummingbirds migrate from South America to the U.S. every year.

Monarch butterflies fly 1,864 miles every year from Canada to Mexico.

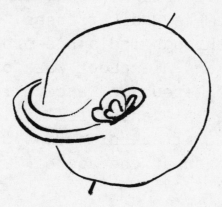

Early explorers navigated by studying the position of the stars, the sun and the moon. The Chinese invented the compass 4,000 years ago. But Europeans didn't start using the compass until 1,000 years ago.

The Phoenicians in 600 BC became the first people to sail around Africa.

Alexander the Great (356-323 BC) led a Greek invasion force to capture Asia and Persia, marched through Syria, Egypt, and Babylon, and founded the city Alexandria in 331 BC. It still stands today on the shores of the Mediterranean. On his way through India his troops rebelled and Alexander was forced to return to Macedonia, a country north of Greece. Alexander fell ill of fever, and after three days of illness died at the age of 33.

Alexander the ill

Alexander the dead

Christopher Columbus was the first European to discover America. The Vikings who were from Norway may have got there before him, and the Native American Indians had  been living there for a long time already. When Columbus reached America in 1492 he mistakenly thought he was in India. In fact, Columbus didn't actually land on what we know as America. He landed in the West Indies, which he mistakenly thought were islands off China.

he was lost!

Roald Amundsen and his team reached the South Pole on December 4, 1911. No other human had made it that far south before. Around the same time, another explorer, Captain Scott, and his crew, died while attempting to reach the Pole.

Amundsen ate his dogs

Ferdinand Magellan proved to everyone that the world was round by sailing around it. You can see the world is round if you hold up a ruler along the horizon on a calm day. The earth's surface will curve. Also, there are two smudges in the sky that you can see on a clear night that are actually other galaxies. These are called the Clouds of Magellan.

Magellan was the first European to discover the Pacific Ocean.

I call it the Pacific Ocean

Marco Polo was an Italian explorer who traveled as far as China with his father and uncle in 1271.

Sir Edmund Hillary was the first person to climb Mount Everest (the highest mountain in the world). Sir Ed, a New Zealander, climbed to the top of the world in 1953 with the sherpa Tenzing Norgay.

Neil Armstrong was the first human to walk on the moon. He is famous for the line "one small step for man; one giant leap for mankind." You can catch a glimpse of Armstrong playing Armstrong in the film *Apollo 13* (starring Tom Hanks), which is about a  failed attempt to land on the moon and a heroic trip back to the earth's atmosphere.

James Cook explored many of
the islands in the Pacific. He
was the first European to land
in New Zealand. Abel Tasman, a
Dutch explorer, was first to see
New Zealand but failed to come
ashore.

Kupe was the first Polynesian to discover New Zealand. There are different versions of the story but one is that he and his wife were out chasing the fish of his ancestors. They were following a giant octopus when they saw New Zealand. At first they thought it was just a long white cloud on the horizon. But when they realized it was land they called it "Aotearoa," which means "land of the long white cloud." This was hundreds, maybe more than a thousand years, before Captain Cook arrived. But no one knows for sure what the date was.

One of Africa's most famous
European explorers was Dr.
Livingstone. He went missing
for five years. He was found by
an American journalist, Henry
Stanley, sent to look for him.
And his first words on finding
the missing Livingstone were: "Dr.
Livingstone, I presume."

what if he liked being missing?

The first person to make a globe
of the world was a German
mapmaker called Martin Behaim.
He made it between 1490 and
1492. It was very inaccurate.

Important Inventions

Who invented paper?

Some time around AD 105 (check out
AD and BC on page 143) a Chinese
guy named Tsai Lun discovered that
a mixture of rags, bark from a
mulberry tree, and hemp poured onto
a screen dried into a sheet. He used
alum to rub the sheet smooth and
found he could draw on it.
Paper making became a specialized
art that was developed further
by the Arabs. The first paper
mill was built in Baghdad, Iraq,
many centuries after Tsai Lun's
experiment with tree bark, hemp, and
rags.
The first page-bound book came out
of the Arab world.

Who invented the wheel?

There are no wheels in nature so early humans couldn't steal the idea from what lay around them. The idea for a wheel may have come from the discovery that the carcass of a heavy animal could be moved by rolling it over a number of logs. But then logs can weigh a lot too, and it would make no sense to carry logs a great distance in order to transport an equally heavy animal carcass.

Bruce or Igor had to develop the idea further. Why not trim the logs to bits of logs? And hey, why not join the two tiny bits of logs by a long stick? Scientists believe that this is how the wheel and axle came into existence.

With the invention of the wheel the first
carts came into use. Travel was now
possible. Before long, roads had to be
built. Romans were famous for building
incredibly long, straight roads. Some still
stand in the UK, under London expressways.
Expressways came only after the invention of
the automobile.
Before the car,
people listened out
for the sound of
horse hooves before
crossing a road.

Skateboards are more recent.

The early history goes like this. In 1958, a guy called Bill
Richards who owned a surf shop in California saw some
kids riding surfboards with wheels attached.
Bill ordered some wheels from a roller skate company and
brought out the "sidewalk surfboard."

In the 1970s the skateboard with the kick tail, an upward
curve at the back, gave the rider better control. Also,
polyurethane wheels replaced the old clay-baked wheels,
offering a smoother ride.

Some Amazing Stuff

enough to cook 6 000 000 000 000 000 000 000 000 legs of lamb in 1/2 a second!

The surface temperature of the sun is 9926.2 degrees Fahrenheit. Your average bath temperature is around 100 degrees Fahrenheit. The normal human body temperature is about 98.6 degrees Fahrenheit.

Our Earth and moon are also 4,500, 000,000 years old, as are most of the meteorites that rain down on us.

woof

Meteorites falling on the Egyptian village of Nahkla killed a dog.

Nobody knows how many stars there are in the world. There are too many to count. It's like trying to guess the number of grains of sand on a beach. Take a punt and guess—and who's going to tell you that you're wrong. Though you may want to think in terms of trillions and zillions rather than millions.

There are eight planets

Same thing with insects. So far, over one million species of insects have been identified by entomologists(the fancy word for people who study insects). But the same entomologists estimate that between 2 and 10 times that number may still be waiting to be discovered.

Your nose can smell
the difference between
4,000 substances.

Junk is turning space into a car
wrecker's yard. In 1997, a report
by NASA counted over 25,000 man-
made objects in space: 8,681 were
currently in orbit, another 16,000
were in a state of decay.

**An average-sized adult has around 18 pounds of fat
on them.**

You have 300 bones in your body
when you're born, but then some
of them join together so that
by the time you're an adult you
only have 208.

And you have 639 muscles.

The heaviest organ in the human body is the liver (3.44 pounds on average).

Humans are the only species who laugh. Fifteen of your facial muscles contract when you laugh. It's said that laughing 100 times is equal to 10 minutes on the rowing machine or 15 minutes on the exercise bike.

Laughing lowers your blood pressure and puts more oxygen into your blood. It also gives your diaphragm and abdominal, leg, facial, and back muscles a workout.

The history of toothpaste is as follows: Once upon a time people used fingers and sticks and crushed bone or egg shell. The early toothbrushes were made out of bristles from the necks of pigs. Nylon brushes weren't invented until 1938.

get this guy off me!

The first toothpaste was made out of powdered bark and flavoring. Around 3000 BC, Egyptians were using toothpaste made of powdered ash. Modern toothpastes were developed in the 1800s—inventors added things like soap and chalk. Fluoride and calcium weren't added to toothpaste until the 1960s and 1980s.

In 1892 the first collapsible toothpaste tube was invented. Fillings for teeth have always been around. They used to be made out of stone chips, resin, gum, gold, or mercury. As early as 700 BC, the Etruscans were making false teeth out of ivory and bone.

The dental chair was patented in 1848. The electric drill was patented in 1875.

In 1846, Dr. William Morton was the first dentist to use anaesthetic to pull out teeth. Novocaine was invented in 1905.

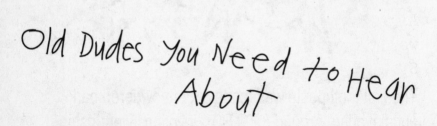

Old Dudes You Need to Hear About

Allah is the Arabic name of the Supreme Being or God.

Aristotle, Pythagoras, Plato,
Archimedes, Hero, Euclid.
Get used to their names. You
will hear more about them at high
school and after. Here's what
they're famous for:

Pythagoras is said to be one of the
greatest mathematicians. He defined
numbers as odd, even, and prime; and
came up with the names to describe
a square and a
triangle.

Archimedes
was born in
Syracuse about
287 BC. Syracuse
is in Sicily,
and Sicily is
that ball-shaped
island that sits
on the toe of
Italy. Check it out on a map.

Archimedes also invented the slingshot. When the Romans attacked Syracuse they thought it would be a breeze. They planned to take over Syracuse in a few days. But thanks to Archimedes' giant sling shots that hurled rocks and darts at the Romans' ships, the battle stretched out to months.

Archimedes came up with five easy ways to move a heavy weight with the least effort:

1. The lever

2. The wheel (see Bruce and Igor on page 43)

3. The pulley

4. The wedge

5. The screw

Charles Darwin (1809-1882), an
Englishman, is famous for his book
On the Origin of Species, which
outlined his idea of how species
evolve over time.

Socrates (c. 470–399 BC) was one of the most famous
teachers ever to have lived. He couldn't
read or write but his best pupil Plato recorded
much of what Socrates taught in his book called the
Dialogues.

Socrates was big on education. All wickedness, he
reckoned, was due to ignorance. The Socratic method
of teaching relied on conversations with his students.
The point of this was to prove that the answers to most
questions lay in people's minds. Socrates was charged
with "corrupting the youth" and sentenced to death. Even
though he had the option, Socrates refused to escape.
Instead, he chose to drink hemlock, a poisonous drug
taken from the plant of the genus Conium.

Plato (c.429–c.347 BC) was famous for writing the **Dialogues**. In his earliest dialogues his old teacher Socrates is a main figure. Plato is also famous for the **Apology,** which records Socrates' defense at his trial. The story goes that Plato was originally named

Aristocles but this was changed to Plato (which means "broad") because of his big forehead and strong body.

Mick Jagger is the leader of a band called The Rolling Stones, the longest surviving rock band in the world. They've been going since the early 1960s. The Rolling Stones' hits include "Satisfaction," "Brown Sugar," "Wild Horses," "Street Fighting Man," "Angie," and heaps more.

The Beatles, the most
famous pop group of all
time, formed in 1959.
The guys in the group
were Paul McCartney, John
Lennon, George Harrison, and
Ringo Starr, and at first
were famous for their mop
haircuts—pretty uncool
now, but not in the early
'60s. Their most famous
records were *Abbey Road*
and *Sergeant Pepper's Lonely
Hearts Club Band*.
Most parents are divided
between being a fan of The
Beatles and a fan of The
Rolling Stones. Not many
love both. Some, but not
many.

John and George are dead now

The pick of your parents' music collection:
Bob Dylan
Bruce Springsteen
Michael Jackson "the King of Pop" *great dancer, but gone a bit weird lately*
James Brown "the godfather of soul"
Madonna
Paul Simon
Jimi Hendrix — 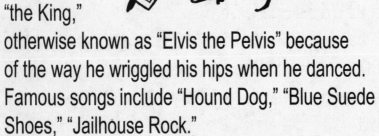 *crazy wild guitarist*
Elvis Presley,
"the King,"
otherwise known as "Elvis the Pelvis" because
of the way he wriggled his hips when he danced.
Famous songs include "Hound Dog," "Blue Suede
Shoes," "Jailhouse Rock."
The Sex Pistols. They were a British band who were
anti everything to do with success and everything
that had gone before them in rock 'n' roll.
They deliberately sang out of tune and with a sneer.
The Monkees were the first made-for-TV band.
They were an invention, which led to the Spice Girls
two decades later.

"Dance of the Sugar Plum Fairy"
is a piece of music written
by the Russian composer Peter
Tchaikovsky. It is part of the
Nutcracker Suite, a ballet that
has a TV version starring Macaulay
Culkin, the little kid from the
movies **Home Alone** and **Home Alone 2**.
"Dance of the Sugar Plum Fairy" is
used a lot in movies and cartoons
including **Ren and Stimpy**.

"Für Elise" ("For Elise") was
written by the German composer
Ludwig van Beethoven for one of his
favorite pupils. Just about anyone
who learns to play the piano will
end up playing this tune. Beethoven
never heard half the music he
composed because he went completely
deaf at the age of 42.

A bit like a champion archer that can't see!

Johann Sebastian Bach applied to the Duke of Brandenburg for a musical job. To show how good he was, Bach composed six amazing concertos and sent them to the Duke. The Duke never opened the envelope, which was only discovered a hundred years later. Now Bach is famous for the Brandenburg Concertos, among other pieces of music.

"Hall of the Mountain King" and "Morning Mood" were written by the Scandinavian Edvard Grieg (born 1843). "Hall of the Mountain King" is very dramatic and is used in comedies on TV as well as an ad for toy trolls. "Morning Mood" is a song that lots of people learn to play when they start learning an instrument. It's also used a lot on TV in air-freshener ads. Both these songs are from Grieg's famous opera called **Peer Gynt**.

The Four Seasons was written by Antonio Vivaldi who lived in Italy. *The Four Seasons* is a group of four concertos based on spring, summer, autumn, and winter. The New Zealand National Bank uses bits and pieces from all these in their TV ads.

most of the classical composers have now decomposed

BLUES is African American in origin. The earliest blues was made up on the spot (improvised), usually sung or played on guitar, banjo or harmonica. Blues today is associated with the 12-bar riff played on guitar. Check out Muddy Waters and B. B. King.

crazy DJ scratching record

HIP-HOP is pretty new on the scene. It covers a broad style including "rap." Nowadays people are more likely to talk about "MC-ing," which is basically the same thing. DJ-ing and "scratching" with records are big in hip-hop culture. Famous hip-hop artists include Eminem and 50 Cent. Eminem's real name is Marshall Mathers. His most famous songs are: "The Real Slim Shady," "Stan," and "One Shot."

POP is short for "popular." So pop music is basically the definition for whatever is trendy or cool to the masses at the moment. The kind of thing that will get airplay for a few weeks max before the next big pop sensation comes along. You know the kind of thing: The Spice Girls and Britney Spears.

HEAVY METAL is loud and fast guitar-based music without a melody. Check out Black Sabbath and Metallica.

JAZZ calls on a combination of wind instruments (like trumpet, saxophone, trombone, clarinet), piano, guitar, drums, vocals. A piece of jazz will often feature solos for each member of the band—which they make up on the spot. There is a huge variety of jazz styles but most jazz has a forward momentum called "sing" and uses "bent" or "blue" notes. Famous jazz musicians include Ella Fitzgerald (singer) and Louis Armstrong (trumpet).

FOLK is used to describe the music of peasants that lasted down through the ages and can't be traced to an original composer. Nowadays it covers a lot more besides. Woody Guthrie is one of the most famous folkies.

DANCE or electronic music covers a lot of styles from "techno," "drum 'n' bass," "hard house," "ambient," "trance," "break-beat," "downbeat" and so on. These types of music basically involve enhancing and developing music through the use of computers and other electronic equipment. Some famous examples include house DJ John Digweed, and the drum 'n' bass DJ Goldie.

OPERA is simply a play that is sung. Usually opera plots are about love and adventure and end in tragedy. Many opera composers lived in Europe and wrote in languages other than English. So, opera is usually sung in Italian, French, or German. Some famous operas include Verdi's *Aida* and Puccini's *Tosca* and *Madame Butterfly*.

CLASSICAL is played by groups of instruments including any of the following: strings, woodwind, brass, & percussion. Mozart, Beethoven, Grieg, Bach are all famous classical composers.

Some more famous people you need to know about to save yourself embarrassment:

Rembrandt was a great Dutch artist famous for his portraits.

Leonardo da Vinci was an inventor, philosopher, artist, and his painting **Mona Lisa** in the Louvre art gallery in Paris is probably the most famous painting in the world. He also designed the first parachute, tank, bicycle, and helicopter.

Michelangelo painted the ceiling in the Sistine Chapel in Rome, Italy, with scenes from the Bible. The ceiling took him 4 years and *The Last Judgement* on the back wall took him 5 years to complete. He also sculpted the massive marble statue of *David*, which is in Florence, Italy.

```
Van Gogh is probably most
famous now as the painter who
cut off his ear. He never sold
a single painting while he
was alive. Now his paintings
sell for millions of dollars.
```

Picasso was a Spanish painter who changed the way we look at things. He had lots of wives and mistresses who used to sit for their portrait. One of his most famous paintings is *Guernica*, a town in Spain that was bombed during the Spanish Civil War in the 1930s.

Andy Warhol? You've heard of pop music. Andy Warhol was a pop artist. He is famous for his paintings of Campbell's soup and screen prints of Marilyn Monroe.

Johann Wolfgang von Goethe (1749–1832) was a German poet, novelist, and playwright.
Among his famous poems is *Prometheus*, which argues that humans must not believe in any Gods but only in themselves.

Shakespeare, James Joyce, Ernest Hemingway, George Orwell, Thomas Mann, Kafka, Anton Chekhov, Leo Tolstoy, Samuel Beckett, Jean-Paul Sartre, Albert Camus, Charlotte Brontë, Jane Austen, and Gertrude Stein are all famous writers.

Katherine Mansfield is famous for her short stories ("The Doll's House" and "The Birthday Party"). New Zealand-born, she spent her adult years in Europe, England mainly, where she hung out with famous writers such as D. H. Lawrence and Virginia Woolf.

Cool Stuff to Impress your Relatives

The wettest place in the world is Meghalaya in Northern India where the average rainfall for the year is 38.94 feet. Also, at Mount Wai 'ale 'ale in Hawaii it rains an average of 350 days per year.
The driest place in the world is the Atacama Desert in Chile, South America, where the average rainfall for a year is 0.02 inches.

The Pacific Ocean is the deepest ocean in the world. At its deepest point it is 6.8 miles. It is also larger than all the world's land masses together.

The largest desert in the world is the Sahara. It covers more than one quarter of Africa. *and it is growing*

Some would say that the Antarctic is the biggest desert—it is bigger than the Sahara, but it is a cold desert: an ice cap.

The world's deepest lake is Lake Baikal in Siberia. It contains 20 percent of the world's unfrozen fresh water.

Ever wondered why fish don't wash up on beaches? It's because fish can sense the tides and undertow of a beach, so they know to swim well clear.

A "flea market" doesn't sell fleas at all. It's a street market that sells secondhand goods.

Second hand fleas

Why is a pineapple called a pineapple? The first Europeans who discovered it thought it looked like a large pine cone and that it tasted like an apple.

When you're hypnotized, you aren't actually asleep. You are completely conscious of your surroundings the whole time. It's like extreme imagining. It's the same as reading a book or watching a movie when you get totally absorbed in the story and you laugh out loud or cry or get scared even though you know it's make-believe.

The first lawnmower was invented in 1830. Lancashire in the UK has the British Lawnmower Museum. Among the things on display are the lawnmowers that belonged to Prince Charles and Princess Diana, a two inch lawnmower, and lawnmowers in use as long ago as in Queen Victoria's reign.

Lawnmower pre 1830...

Grass has inspired one of the best-known lines in poetry:
"I believe a leaf of grass is no less than the journey-work of the stars."
This is from Walt Whitman's *Leaves of Grass,* which is probably the most famous book of poetry ever published with "grass" in the title.

The first clothes buttons were made out of shell and bone. The earliest such buttons go back to 3000 BC. The Greeks and Romans started to make loops for the buttons to pass through. But, button holes didn't appear until the 13th century. Around this time buttons were an expensive luxury and a way of showing off.
In the 17th century Puritans said buttons were "sinful" because they were too showy.

a sinful button

The tuatara is the oldest lizard in the world and is found only in New Zealand. It existed when dinosaurs were around and it has three eyes. The third eye is in the middle of its forehead and has a transparent scale covering it. When the tuataras are young they can distinguish light from dark with their extra eye. But as they grow older their scales and skin grow over it.

Weird food that people eat: wichetty grub— a fat insect (Australia), monkey's brains and bull penis (Asia), camel's feet (France), Mountain Oysters—the testicles of a sheep (New Zealand), and drunken shrimp swimming in a bowl of red wine (Japan).
Hot turtle's blood is drunk with whisky in Korea. Some people in China eat the hands of gorillas; but this is illegal.

72

A blue whale's heart is the size of a small car and weighs as much as eight adult humans. An earthworm has 10 hearts.

Tarantulas live up to 20 years.

Lungfish can live for four years without food or water. This is something it has learnt to do over the years so that the hot, dry deserts where it lives are bearable. So during the dry season it buries itself in the ground and covers itself in this mucus which keeps it moist. Sometimes it comes up for air. This process is called "estivation." It's like hibernation but backwards.

lungfishing in the desert

 The electric eel is not actually an eel. It is just a long, regular fish that happens to be electric (it can give you a 400 volt shock). The South American electric eel can knock out a horse from nine feet away.

The first Homo sapiens (early modern humans) appeared on earth 200,000 years ago and fossils have been found in Africa of Homo sapiens that are about 160,000 years old. But cockroaches have existed for about 300 million years.

The following are known as Fibonacci numbers:
1,1,2,3,5,8,13,21,34,55,89...
Work out the sequence: (0+1=1, 1+1=2, 1+2=3, 2+3=5, 3+5=8, 5+8=13, 8+13=21,13+21=34, 21+34=55, 34+55=89)
Flowers always have a Fibonacci number of petals and the seeds of sunflowers are arranged according to Fibonacci numbers.

Ever wondered how pop groups get their names?
Here's some examples:
The Pogues (1982-96) originally
Pogue Mahone, Irish for pog mo
thon "kiss my arse."

Police (1977-1986): the group's
drummer was the son of a CIA officer.

UB40 (from 1978...) UB40 is a British unemployment
form.

The Rolling Stones took their
name from the Muddy Waters song
"Rollin' Stone."

Oasis is named after a sports center in Swindon, England.

Limp Bizkit—apparently, front man
Fred Durst had a dog, called Bizkit
who limped a lot.

The Doors—Jim Morrison and
organ player Ray Manzarek
named the band after Aldous
Huxley's book, *The Doors of
Perception*.

Foo Fighters—named after a
slang expression used in
World War II by U.S. pilots
to describe the alien-looking
fireballs they saw over Germany.

REM—stands for a state of sleep
called "rapid eye movement"—the
time when you are dreaming.

"Canned laughter" ????????
Canned beans, canned soup,
sure. But canned
laughter? "Canned
laughter" is pre-
recorded laughter
you hear on TV comedies that
has been recorded. That is,
there is no live audience.
Just some pretend nonsense.

Why do your hands prune up when
soaked in water?
The tips of your fingers and toes are covered
in extra thick skin. When soaked for a long
time they absorb water and the skin expands.
But because there is no room for the skin to
expand the skin buckles and gets that prune
look.

canned laughter is not funny

77

Why is the grass green and the
sky blue and roses red?
The grass is green because it contains a green
substance called chlorophyll. The sky is blue
because of the billions of particles in the air that
bounce back the sunlight and make it appear blue.
Roses are red because they are crafty–they are red
to attract bees so they can be pollinated.

How does a lightbulb work?
Simple. It contains a tungsten
wire that when heated by
electricity glows. The wire
or filament has to be tungsten
because it remains solid at high
temperatures. When the lightbulb
doesn't work anymore it is because
the filament has slowly vaporized.

Why don't spiders stick to their webs?
Because not all parts of the spider's web are sticky and the spider knows where to step.

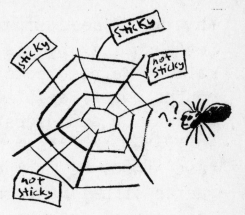

Bats live in caves because they are nocturnal-meaning they sleep during the day and are active at night. They need somewhere dark to hang out during daylight hours. So a cave is just the thing.

When you blush the blood rushes to your face, telling you and the world, "Hey, I'm embarrassed."

Why do we need spit?

Let's call it by its real name—
saliva. We need saliva to keep our
mouths moist; spit also helps us
to swallow and digest food. And it
activates the taste buds so we can
taste food. We produce about two
quarts of saliva each day.
In Tanzania, the Masai tribe
considers spitting to be a sign of
goodwill. The Masai spit on newborn
babies to bring them luck in life.

Why are tears salty?

It's because our eyes are covered
in a weak salt jelly called a
vitreous, which helps to protect
our eyes. Our tears are just a
run-off of that. By the way, salt
does not change the taste of food.
It makes your taste glands more
sensitive.

The reason why we have eyelashes is to protect our eyes. Camels have seriously long eyelashes because they have to cope with sandstorms in the desert.

Why do we get freckles?
Actually they are just areas of skin that tan easier than others.

Hair is tricky stuff. It looks longer after people die when, in fact, it just looks longer because the body shrinks from dehydration.

Dead people can be used to make rope

But what about whiskers?
Have you ever wondered what's the
point? Men still get hair over
their faces because back in prehistoric times
people had hair all
over to keep them
warm. Facial hair
is another one of
those souvenirs
from an earlier
age.

Warm
hairy
person

Why do we blink?
It's just a reflex we are born with. When we blink
a film of water cleans our eyes. Think of your
eyelashes as windshield wipers.

Why can't we tickle ourselves?
Because we know it's coming.

Why do we laugh?

It's just another way of letting go of the emotions. Our laugh is inherited. So if you bray like a donkey it should be easy to figure out which parent to blame.

On that subject, you must know why you look like your mom and dad. Every person and animal, from dingoes to snakes and lions, contain DNA that has instructions on how we look. A parrot looks like a parrot because of its DNA coding. Same with an elephant. You and me look like we do because of our DNA code. If your hair is black it's because of the DNA code you inherited from your parents.

I look nothing like Mum and Dad

DNA is the miraculous chemical substance found in all living things. Three scientists working in England called Francis Crick, James Watson, and Maurice Wilkins worked out how DNA works in 1953. DNA is a recipe for building, running, and reproducing a plant, animal, or microbe.

Why don't we live until we are 200? Our bodies, like cars, grow too old. A French woman, Jeanne Calment, lived to be 122. She was born before the first airplane and lived long enough to see the pictures of the first man to step on to the moon.

Why can't you see in the dark? The retina in our eye can only let in a certain amount of light so when it's dark no images are sent through to our brain.

There are stories about dolphins steering shipwrecked sailors to shore. So what about cats? Have cats done anything heroic in history? There's this. In 1483, Sir Henry Wyatt was captured and imprisoned by King Richard III. While he was starving to death he made friends with a stray cat that brought him pigeons, which kept him alive until he was released.

Why do cats have whiskers?

Whiskers are sensory devices. They send messages to the cat's brain like alien ships sending messages back to their home planet. It helps them to move quickly in the dark. Whiskers can also sense movement of smaller things, such as mice.

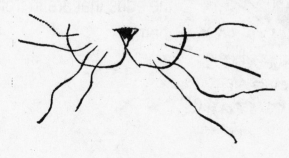

How come dogs need baths but cats don't?
Dogs can roll around in the dirt all day long and feel good about it. Cats like to clean themselves. They use their raspy tongues to clean their fur. Their tongues pull out dead fur and remove dirt and dust.

How come hens don't squash their eggs when they sit on them?
It's a trick. They don't actually sit on the eggs but sit behind them and puff out their breast feathers to cover the eggs that are in front of them.

chicken
inventing
wheel by
mistake!

Some dangerous animals to look out for

(most of them live in Africa and Australia):

The stonefish is the world's most poisonous fish. It looks like a stone and has an ugly spine. If you stand on it, it can kill you.

The box jellyfish lives off the coast of northern Australia and is the most poisonous sea creature in the world. You can die within a few minutes if you touch its tentacles, which are sometimes more than two yards long.

The funnel web spider-which also
lives in Oz and is usually found in
someone's house-can bite through a
finger nail.

There are piranhas that can gobble
up a horse in minutes but what
most people don't realize is that
most piranhas are
vegetarian.

are you a
Vegetable?

Over 2,000,000 people are bitten
by snakes every year and more than
50,000 die from snake bites. The
snakes that bite most people are the
Asian cobras, but they aren't the
most poisonous.

Elephants are usually gentle giants, but if annoyed by
humans they will go into a blind trampling rage.

The great white shark isn't the largest shark but it is definitely the angriest.

Cape buffalo don't eat people (they're herbivores) but they do see humans as a threat so will run and charge at people with their large horns.

There are a few different types of crocodile but the most dangerous is the Australian salt water crocodile.

Shrews are like tiny mice with long noses. Many of them die of old age when they reach only one year old.

Shrews are almost the most angry and hungriest animals in the world- they are constantly killing and eating things. Often they will eat their own weight in food in just three hours and they will die if they don't eat for one day. Their spit is poisonous and is similar to cobra venom, but since they are so small they can only kill other small creatures like mice and frogs. Their hearts beat a thousand times a minute!

Killer bees are the result of an experiment that went wrong when Brazilian scientists tried to breed a new type of honey bee in the 1950s. Unfortunately, the new bees escaped and bred with the wild honey bees of Brazil. And while their stings aren't as powerful as regular bees, they travel in packs and turn angry very easily. Killer bees will chase you for more than 300 yards and then attack you without stop for up to 10 hours.

Grrr

Some plants are carnivores too. It's true! There are more than 6,000 types. They usually eat insects but sometimes will eat a small fish and even small rodents, birds, and frogs. These victims tend to be sick or dying and therefore make for an easy target.

There was once a man who had athlete's foot (which is a disease where fungus grows on your foot) and he fed parts of his decaying foot to his pet Venus Fly Trap (a type of carnivorous plant) and it ate it.

One more interesting plant: the Katemfe plant grows in Africa and is 6,150 times as sweet as sugar!

A giant guinea pig lived in South America about 8 million years ago. It was as big as a cow and weighed one whole ton (2,000 pounds).

Guinea piggus massivis

Did you know that temperature affects the sex of some animals?

Take the case of turtles. When the mother is ready to lay her eggs she swims ashore and digs a large hole in the sand to lay her eggs. Now, before the eggs are buried they don't know if they are boy or girl eggs. This is where temperature comes into it.

The temperature has to be between 78.8°F and 93.2°F for the eggs to hatch at all. At the warmer end the eggs will hatch girl turtles and at the colder end, all boy turtles. At the middle of the range, the eggs will hatch an even amount of boy and girl turtles.

Temperature has a similar effect on alligator eggs. Only the opposite happens—more girl alligators if the temperature is colder and vice versa. BUT, alligators can actually choose if they want girls or not. If the mother decides she wants girls she will lay her eggs down in the marsh where it's wetter and colder. If she wants boys she will lay her eggs in a nice dry and warm place.

There are some animals that can be either male or female. The blue headed wrasse fish hangs out in groups of females with one male as leader. But when the male dies or is eaten the strongest female blue headed wrasse slowly turns into a male. The process takes about a week. After she has turned into a he all the other blue headed wrasses in the group have forgotten everything that was before.

Worms, snails,
and some fish
such as the
cuttlefish
and jellyfish
can change to
male or female
whenever they
feel like it.

though who
tell the difference
could

Communes were popular in the 1960s
when young people tried to come up
with a new way of living.
It often meant a whole lot of *hippies*
families sharing the same house or
property or maybe a bunch of single
people or couples living together
in a self-sufficient way by growing
their own vegetables and fruit.

The weaver bird lives in South Africa. Sometimes
it will build a nest that is two or three yards high
and will share it with up to 100 other weaver bird
families.

More interesting inventions

The earliest school textbook that has been discovered is from around 3500 BC and comes from the Sumerian city of Erech. The textbook is in the form of several hundred clay tablets containing word lists to be studied and memorized.

Braille was invented in 1824 by a 15-year-old boy Louis Braille who was blind from the age of three.

The first printed book was the Gutenberg Bible and this was published in Germany in 1454. Only 300 copies were printed, using moveable metal type. Up until then manuscripts were copied out by hand–often by monks. There are 45 copies still in existence today.

Some say the first daily newspaper came out in Germany in 1615. It was called the **Frankfurter Zeitung**. Yet others point to the Dutch **Nieuve Tijdinghe** in 1605. And you can even go back further. **The Acta Diurna (Action Journal)** was published on a daily basis in Rome around 59 BC. It carried the usual stuff on sports and local court events. The Chinese also had a hand-printed court circular doing the rounds during the 7th century Tiang Dynasty.

The first pens?
How about a finger dipped into the juice of a berry or sometimes blood. By this method prehistoric people were able to write symbols on themselves or over the walls of their caves.

After the finger, came the twig. The first pen-like instruments came about with the first writing. The earliest evidence of both go back as far as 3000 BC in Sumer. Sumerian scribes also used sharp twigs to etch into wet clay tablets that they baked in ovens.

The first real pens appeared in Egypt 3000–2800 BC. These were reeds with a hollow center, called a stylus that could contain a color liquid.

Steelpoint pens showed up in England in 1780.

Fountain pens were so-called because their ink flowed continuously like water in a fountain.

The ballpoint pen was invented by John Loud in America in 1888. The ballpoint contained a rotating ball that distributed ink evenly.

Lazlo Biro, a Hungarian living in Argentina during World War Two, was responsible for modernizing the ballpoint pen. That's why ballpoint pens are sometimes called BIROs.

When were pencils discovered? Back in the 1500s a bunch of trees were blown over in England and unearthed a deposit of substance which at the time was thought to be lead. Two hundred years later it was discovered that the stuff was a form of carbon. It was given the name graphite after the Greek word meaning "to write." The first pencil was a hunk of graphite wrapped in sheepskin. The next step was a major event in the development of the pencil. A stick of cedar was hollowed out and a piece of graphite was stuck down the hollow. The next step saw a groove cut into the wood, the graphite was laid along the groove then a section of wood was stuck on top to enclose the graphite. These days, pencil lead is a mix of finely ground graphite and clay mixed with water and pressed together at high temperatures into thin rods.

The eraser is a pretty recent event. A hundred years ago teachers felt erasers would only encourage kids to make mistakes.

Nowadays 14 billion pencils are produced in the world each year, enough pencils to circle the earth 62 times.

If you ask your mom or dad to name the invention that has saved the most lives they will most likely say it is penicillin. And penicillin has saved millions of lives… BUT, you can blow their socks off with a different answer.

What about the curved glass that we call a lens?

They will argue about this. BUT … point this out to them.

Without a lens there could be no microscope, and therefore, no way of studying the bacteria that have wiped out millions of people around the planet.

Photography would not have been invented without the discovery of the lens. Millions more wouldn't be able to read because without glasses they wouldn't be able to see the letters.

Ask your old man who invented
glasses. He probably won't know.
Not many people do. More people
probably know that Bill
Bass is a sunglasses
brand name than those who
know the name of Salvino
D'Armato. He was the Italian guy
who invented glasses around the
year 1285.

It's amazing how many things have been discovered by
accident.
A German guy called Hans Lippershey who made
spectacles for a living happened to discover the
magnifying power of two lenses when he accidentally put
one in front of the other. He happened to have the steeple
of a distant church in his focus. The effect of the two
lenses doubled up was to bring the steeple closer.
This started a series of experiments which resulted in the
invention of the telescope.

About now, you need to
hear about Gallileo. In
1609, Gallileo built an
incredibly powerful telescope
and pointed it up at the
night sky. For the first
time it was possible to see
a number of moons around
the planet Jupiter and the
distant rings of Saturn.
Gallileo enjoyed observing
the Sun and one day he
noticed all these dark spots
on it. He called them "sun
spots" and decided that they
were areas on the Sun that
are cooler. Eventually he
went blind, which was
probably from staring at
the Sun all the time.

The invention of the microscope came about 100 years later, although scientists aren't sure who invented it.

Another Italian, Marcello Malpighi, was the first man to see blood coursing through the network of lungs. Marcello was the first man to accurately describe the process of respiration

yeehaa
I am breathing!

(Respiration, dummies, is another word for breathing) in the human body.

"Frigidus" is Latin for cold by the way. That's how we get the name fridge. But how do fridges keep the milk cold? In modern fridges there is an evaporating substance that changes from gas to liquid and back again, and it steals all the heat particles from the milk to make it go cold.

Who invented hamburgers?

It's hard to say since there are no monuments or biographies to go on. And no movies have been made on the inventor of the hamburger. What we do know is this. Hamburgers take their name from Hamburg in Germany, which is a bit misleading for some people who have never eaten a hamburger. They would reasonably expect there to be ham in it. German immigrants to America in the 1850s introduced the hamburger. Does the credit for its invention go to one person? Or a group of people, like the group who supposedly wrote the Bible? No one knows for sure. In any case, hamburgers are like pizza, an age-old recipe handed down through the generations.

The first pizzeria in America opened in 1905.

Why are bananas called bananas? They are named after a place in Zaire, Africa, where bananas flourish.

What are marshmallows made of? Marshmallows originated as a medical syrup and ointment from the root sap of marshmallow, sugar, and egg white. Nowadays they are made of corn syrup, dextrose, gelatine and something called egg albumen. Gross fact: Americans eat about 90 million pounds of marshmallows each year-in other words, about the same weight as 1,286 grey whales.

to many marshmallows will do this!

Jellybeans are more historic.
Jellybeans are thought to be a descendent of Turkish delight, which is a Middle Eastern sweet that goes back to biblical times. Turkish delight and jellybeans have the same soft centers. In C. S. Lewis's **The Lion, the Witch and the Wardrobe** a boy is enticed to turn against his sister and brother in Narnia after he eats magic Turkish delight given to him by the White Witch.

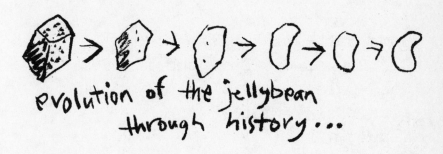

evolution of the jellybean through history...

have a test cake

No single genius invented biscuits or cookies. Biscuit historians tell us they were invented by accident. Early bakers used small amounts of cake batter to test their oven temperatures before baking the final cake. These little "test cakes" were called "koekje," which means "little cake" in Dutch. If you say "koekje" out loud it sounds close to "cookie." And that's no surprise because the Dutch arrived in America with their "koekjes" and their language around the 1600s.

Some soft-drink history:
Dr. Pepper was invented in 1885
Coca-Cola® in 1886
Pepsi-Cola® in 1898
7-up® in 1929
Diet Pepsi® in 1964
Soft drinks came in glass bottles until aluminum cans were introduced in 1960.

Who invented chewing gum?

People living around the shores of the Mediterranean used to chew the sap and gum off trees for the taste and to get rid of bad breath. In Greece and the Middle East people have chewed mastic gum for centuries. This is a resin collected off the bark of the mastic tree. It sweetens the breath and cleans teeth.

Up until World War II gum was made of chicle mixed with flavors. Chicle was a kind of rubber so it was like chewing the end of your gumboot. After World War II scientists found a way to make a gum base without using chicle.

The urge to chew apparently begins with breast-feeding. Then as you get older you might choose to chew a grass blade or straw end.

Here are some important gum dates. In 1893, William Wrigley gave the world spearmint and juicy fruit flavors. In 1928, modern bubble gum came on to the market. In the 1930s, baseball cards were included with packets of gum.

Sugarless gum came on to the market in the 1950s. On July 19, 1994, Susan Williams from Fresno, California, blew the largest bubble ever blown–it was 23 inches in diameter. (Check out the *Guinness Book of Records* 1995).

Embarrassment tip: to remove gum from your hair rub it with peanut butter.

Weirdo tip: it's illegal to import, manufacture, or sell gum in Singapore.

International information: gum in Swedish is "tuggumi." In Portugese it is "pastilka elastica." In Chinese it is "leung how chu."

The origins of ice cream can be
traced back to the 4th century BC.
The Roman Emperor Nero (AD 37-68)
used to order ice to be brought back
from the mountains and combined with
fruit toppings.
King Tang (AD 618-97) of
Shang, China, created an ice
and milk concoction. And in
fact, historians seem to think
that ice cream arrived in
Europe from China. Over time
different recipes were made up.
It's known that ice cream arrived
in the U.S. in the 1700s. George
Washington enjoyed it as a dessert,
so did Thomas Jefferson.
The first ice cream parlor opened in
New York City in 1776.
In 1851, a guy in Baltimore,
Maryland, named Jacob Fussell
established the first large-scale
ice-cream plant.
In 1897, the modern ice-cream scoop
was invented by Alfred L. Cralle.

The edible cone made its debut at the 1904 St. Louis World Fair.
A year before an Italian man living in the U.S.A. invented an edible cup with a handle. Prior to the invention of the edible cone, paper and metal cups were used for ice cream in England and Europe.

Originally the Eskimo Pie was called the "I-Scream-Bar." The first Eskimo Pie chocolate-covered ice cream appeared in 1934—after an ice-cream shop owner saw a young customer undecided between buying a chocolate bar or an ice cream sandwich. The shop owner, Chris Nelson, thought, "Why not combine the two?" The rest is history.

Have you ever wondered about the weirdness of Häagen-Dazs as a brand name for ice cream? The story is, Reuben Mattus, an American born in Poland, came up with the Häagen-Dazs name because he thought it sounded Danish.

The word for ice cream in German is "Eiscreme."

The French word is "crème glacée."

In Italian it's "il gelato."

In Dutch "ijsco."

Sweaty stinky stuff

Old socks. There is a reason why they smell the way they do. It's because of the sweat that comes off our feet. Sweat is just salt and water, and it's not that which stinks. Bacteria is attracted to the sweat and will actually eat it. It is excretions from the bacteria that cause that whiff when you take off your shoes.

Your feet are the sweatiest part of your body. Each foot contains over 250,000 sweat glands.

In one day, each foot can produce more than a pint of water.

So why do we sweat in the first place if we just end up dumping it in our socks and stuff?
Sweating allows the body to cool as water evaporates. But when the bacteria on your skin get to it and cause the smell, that's where soap and water come into the picture.

We have about 2.6 million sweat
glands in our skin. This is where
the sweat is made. There are two
types of sweat gland:

1   eccrine gland (palms, soles of
    feet and forehead).

2   apocrine gland (armpits and
    groin areas). These are the
    larger sweat glands which
    start working when you reach
    the age of 10, 11, 12, 13, 14.

And we have another sweat gland
which is a kind of version of the
apocrine gland. This gland is
in our ears and makes ear wax.
Useful, huh?
Ear wax, by the way, is supposed
to protect our ears from things
such as dust, fluff, and insects.

Stuff to impress your kid brother and sister with...

intestines straightened

"Misnomer" is the word we use to describe those things that aren't really what they say they are. For example: the small intestine in the human body is 22 feet long and the large intestine is only five feet long.

long

Chow mein is a Chinese dish of fried noodles with shredded meat or shrimps and vegetables

small

The sandwich was invented by the cook to the 4th Earl of Sandwich. The Earl loved to gamble. He loved it so much he wouldn't leave his game to eat. So his cook buttered two slices of bread and stuck a thick slice of meat between the bread and gave it to the Earl. Abracadabra-the sandwich was born.

114

The Club Sandwich is a term for a three-decker sandwich.

You may have wondered where the word Abracadabra comes from? Magicians mutter it, don't they? Just before they pull a rabbit out of a hat. But the word goes back to the 2nd century AD when it was thought to be a word containing magical powers. Amulets inscribed with "abracadabra" were worn around the neck and supposed to offer the wearer protection against fever.

abracadabra

Another weird saying, "open sesame," pops up in "Ali Baba and the Forty Thieves," one of the most popular stories from the *Arabian Nights*.

Ali Baba hides up a tree as a band of robbers enter a secret cave by saying the magic words "open sesame." When the robbers leave, Ali repeats the words and gets inside the cave where he finds a mountain of treasure. He carries off some of the gold but his brother Cassim is not so lucky. Once inside the cave he forgets the magic word "sesame" and says "open wheat, open barley…" to the door, but of course the door stays shut. He is found by the thieves who kill him.

The longest word in English is "pneumonoultramicroscopicsilico-volcanoconiosis" to describe a lung disease caused by inhaling silica dust.

The average human body contains enough iron to make a three inch nail, enough sulphur to kill all the fleas on a dog, enough carbon to make 900 pencils, enough fat to make seven bars of soap, and enough water to fill a ten gallon tank.

The average person has as much hair as a hairy primate only it is shorter and finer hair.
Each hair on our scalp has a life-span of three years. Eyelashes have a life span of 150 days.
We blink every 2-10 seconds. A baby does not blink at all in the first few months of its life.

unless you are one of these:

Our brain uses up more energy than any other organ (one fifth of all the food we eat). Seventy-five percent of the brain is water.

They called John von Neumann "the fastest brain in the west." At age four he could talk to his father in ancient Greek. At age eight he memorized 44 huge books and could multiply eight figures by eight figures in his head. Later, as a scientist, he was the first man to attach a TV screen to a computer.

eeek!

Just as each one of us has a unique finger print, we each have a unique tongue print.

You use 17 muscles to smile and 43 muscles to frown.

The average person has over 1,460 dreams a year.

We die with the same brain cells we are born with. All other tissues, such as muscles, kidney, bones, teeth, and blood are replaced from time to time.

Food passes through the small intestine in two hours—it takes about 14 hours to get through the large intestine. So the time it takes from when you eat a hamburger to when it comes out the other end is about the same time it takes to fly from Sydney to New York.

Our noses remain the same size our whole lives as when we were born but our eyes and ears keep on growing.

The tallest man ever was Robert Pershing Wadlow born in 1918. By the time he was 8 years old he was six feet two inches and weighed 195 pounds. He went to become the world's biggest boy scout at seven feet, four inches when he was just 13 years old. He ended up growing to eight feet, eleven inches and at the time of his death, he weighed 438 pounds.

Isaac Newton was famous for inventing the laws of motion and gravity. In 1816 his tooth sold for 730 pounds (about $3,250 today) and was bought by an English nobleman who had the tooth set in a ring.

The most valuable lock of hair sold at auction belonged to Elvis Presley. The lock of hair was sold by his personal hairdresser for $115,120.

A "hair breadth" as in "he was a hair breadth away from being hit from behind by the golf ball" is officially 1/48 of an inch.

The first roads came about from early humans following animal tracks. The ancient Romans were first to construct roads. They created over 52,988 miles of roads fanning out from Rome.

A Scottish blacksmith Kirkpatrick MacMillan invented the bike in 1839. Early bikes were called "bone-shakers" because the metal-rimmed tires shuddered with every bump in the road. In 1876, a London inventor called Archibald Sharp invented the spoked wheel. Soon after, John Dunlop introduced the air-filled tire.

my idea: square wheels for steps

The fastest animal in the world is the peregrine falcon, which can fly at 186 miles per hour.

The cheetah is the fastest land animal. It has been recorded as traveling at speeds of 70 miles per hour in pursuit of its prey.
Check out the rest of the speed merchants:
The prong horn antelope can run up to speeds of 61 miles per hour.

The greyhound	39
A rabbit	38
Giraffe	35
Humans	26
Pig	11
Chicken	9

The slowest land animal is the
South American sloth. It travels
at about .06–.09 miles per hour
so it takes an hour to cover a
distance of 328–525 feet. Sloths
are so slow that moss grows over
them. This is pretty clever
because it means that their main
enemies (harpy eagles and jaguars)
hardly ever see them.

A frigate bird's skeleton weighs less than its
feathers.

It's a tough world for a lot of
animals. But before you start
feeling sorry for them, think
about what Voltaire, a famous
French writer and philosopher, had
to say on the subject.
"There are two things for which
animals are to be envied: they
know nothing of future evils, or
of what people say about them."

Stuffed toy animals though have
a cushier life. They hang around
on beds and get patted a lot.
And NEVER go hungry.

The first teddy bear was made by a sweet shop owner and his wife in New York some time around 1902.
Morris Mitchom and his wife came up with the idea after seeing a cartoon of the American President Teddy Roosevelt with a gun in his hand while refusing to shoot a bear cub.

Winnie the Pooh in the books by A. A. Milne is probably the world's most famous bear. Winnie always has his paws in a honey pot. He is pretty thick at times but he also has lots of good friends such as Tigger, Kanga, Roo, Eeyore, Christopher Robin, and Piglet.
Paddington Bear is a smarter bear. Paddington Bear was found at Paddington Station in London, with a half-eaten jar of marmalade and a photo of his Aunt Lucy lost in Peru, and with a note around his neck saying, "Please look after this bear." The Paddington Bear books are written by Michael Bond.

Polar bears can smell the
rotting carcass of a dead seal
from 18.64 miles away.
*Dogs can smell the body of a
person 26 feet under water.*

The Chicago Bears
are a team in the
National Football
League.

*they eat the
other teams!*

The hamster was the first rodent to become
a household pet. The hamster's offspring are
born only 16 days after the female hamster
gets pregnant.

Canaries are birds named after the Canary Islands. They spread through Europe after the Spanish conquered the islands in the 15th century. For a while, the Spanish actually controlled the canary's population by selling only the male bird. In England, miners used to take a canary underground whenever there was a risk of explosion or deadly gas. Bad fumes such as carbon monoxide would quickly overwhelm the canary and so if the bird was affected the miners knew to get out of there as quickly as possible. If a baby sparrow is reared by a canary it may sing like a canary.

Some birds have two voice boxes which enable them to sing two songs at the same time. Starlings, tuis, and Australian magpies have two voice boxes (or syrinxes), which makes their songs very hard to imitate.

fly like an eagle

bye bye

blackbird

Cats have always had an easy time
of it. Even in ancient times cats
were pampered. In ancient Egypt
cats were protected by law from
injury and death. A cat's death
was mourned by the whole family.
Sometimes the grieving owner would
embalm their cats, wrap them in
the finest linen and put them in
mummy cases made from bronze and
wood. The reason for their special
status was because they were
thought to be the embodiment of
the gods. The Egyptian cat goddess
is called "Bastet."
In Europe cats enjoyed the same
armchair ride. In AD 948 a prince
stated that a kitten cost the
equivalent of a penny before its
eyes opened; and after it caught
its first mouse its price doubled.

The first cat show was staged in Britain's famous Crystal Palace in 1871. It was called Crystal Palace because it was made of glass.

CATS is a famous musical comedy by Andrew Lloyd Webber (first staged in 1981) based on poems from the famous poet T. S. Eliot's **Old Possum's Book of Practical Cats** (1939).

Some cats, long given up as dead, have found their way home from a distance of 1,800 miles.

But dogs are our oldest companions. Records show that dogs were household pets more than 14,000 years ago–long before anyone really knew about canaries, goldfish, and even cats. When you think about it, the world wouldn't have been comfortable enough yet for cats to move in.

Things we say without really thinking about

"Dead from the neck up" means someone who's really stupid.

"Sleep tight" refers to when the old rope beds needed to be tightened. To sleep tight was to sleep without having to get out of bed to tighten the ropes.

"Tie the knot" is another expression for getting married. It refers to tying the rope knots of the marriage bed.

A bad mood is sometimes attributed to "getting out the wrong side of the bed this morning." This refers to an old superstition where it was bad luck to put your left foot down first when getting out of bed.

"Mind your own beeswax." In the old days small pox caused the face to pock and women would fill these pock marks with beeswax. On hot days the beeswax sometimes melted. So another would point out "mind your own beeswax."
Today the saying is used when we want to tell someone to mind their own business.

"The clink" is another term for jail. This name comes from the prison in Clink Street in Southwark, London, in the 1700s.

We say "spend a penny" when we mean to "take a leak" but it actually refers to an early version of a pay toilet (that cost a penny to use).

Why do we say we're feeling "under the weather" when we're feeling like crap? It's a nautical term used by the British navy in the 1800s. When a sailor was ill he was kept below decks or "under the weather."

"TLC" means "tender loving care."

"BLT" is a bacon, lettuce and tomato sandwich. Get it right, brothers and sisters.

A "white elephant" is something that cost a heap and is basically useless. In the late 1800s a circus promoter named P. T. Barnum bought a white elephant from India. When the elephant was shipped across to the U.S. it turned out not to be a white elephant but an elephant covered in pink splotches.

"Shut your face." This is an old one. It harks back to the days of knights in shining armor who wore face plates for extra protection. If you shut your face you couldn't talk.

"POSH." No, not the Spice Girl. When we say someone looks posh in their expensive clothes we are using a word that goes back to a time when people sailed between England and India. The most expensive cabins were the shaded ones facing north. POSH stands for "port outwards" and "starboard home."

"Money for old rope." This is a cheerful one. The phrase means money that comes to you easily and dates back to the days of public hangings. The hangman always got to keep the rope. The rope was also popular with the crowds. So after the hanging, the hangman would cut up the rope and sell portions of it.

To "check out the plumbing" is to go to the toilet.

it is definitely blocked!

A "chicken and egg situation" is used to describe a problem where it's not clear which of two things caused the other to happen. For example, what came first: the chicken or the egg?

"Cold enough to freeze the balls off a brass monkey." It makes no sense, does it? On war ships the cannon balls were made of iron and the plate they were stored on beside the cannon was made of brass. This brass plate was known as a "monkey." In extreme cold, the two metals would react to the cold differently and the iron balls would fall off the monkey.

Some more old English phrases include "chew the fat," which means having a talk with someone. Hosts used to offer their visitors a piece of bacon fat to chew on while they warmed themselves before the fire. Another phrase is to "wet your whistle," which means to quench your thirst. In the old English taverns the tankards used to have a whistle on them for the customers to blow when they needed a refill.

Here's another from the old English pub. "Mind your P's and Q's." P's and Q's refers to Pints and Quarts. A customer would indicate whether he or she wanted a pint or a quart of beer by the angle at which they held their elbow. So, if you only had money for a pint you'd want to make sure your elbow angle didn't indicate you wanted a quart. "Minding your P's and Q's" is another way of telling yourself to be careful in an accurate sort of way.

"Come the raw prawn" is a neat Australian expression for when someone is trying to pull the wool over your eyes, i.e., trick you. It makes all the more sense if you happen to know that a raw prawn is hard to swallow.

To "come up smelling of roses" is to come out of a difficult experience in one piece.

"Carrot and stick" refers to having two choices. You'll be given a carrot if you move. If you don't you will be given the stick.

"Big Brother" is the bossy leader in George Orwell's book *1984* who makes himself the know-it-all boss of everyone.

"Big Ben" is the famous bell attached to the Westminster Clock standing in the Houses of Parliament in London. Big Ben weighs 13 ½ metric tons (29,762 pounds).

Cat burglar is a thief who enters a building by climbing in through a window like a cat.

"Catch-22" means a "no-win situation." Whatever choice you make, you will either lose or be in trouble. **Catch-22** is the name of a famous novel.

"Chill out" means to take things easy.

Sometimes you come across a date given as c.1823. Ever wondered about the c? It stands for "circa," which

means "about" or "around." It's used
when the exact dates aren't known.

A general knowledge question:
Which TV cartoon character said
these things:

"I'm glad we're stranded. It'll be just like the Swiss
Family Robinson–only, with more cursing!"

And this–
"Part of
this D-minus
belongs to
God."

And this–"Man, I wish I was an adult so I could
break the rules."

The answer is our friend and ally from Springfield, Bart Simpson.

Who invented underpants?
It's a long story that leads all the way to long johns but starts out with the simple loin cloth. Don't 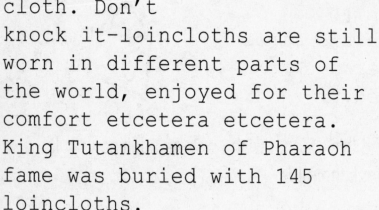 knock it-loincloths are still worn in different parts of the world, enjoyed for their comfort etcetera etcetera. King Tutankhamen of Pharaoh fame was buried with 145 loincloths.

Women's bras are a more recent
story. In 1913, a New York woman
by the name of Mary Phelps Jacob
stitched together the first bra
by tying two handkerchiefs with
ribbon. She made these things for
family and friends. A year later
she had a patent for her design.
Another woman, Amelia Jenks
Bloomer, invented the loose
trouser-like
undies called
bloomers.
The modern
Y-front men's
briefs were
sold for the
first time
in Chicago on
January 19, 1935. The company who
made them called them "Jockeys"
after the jockstrap. The company
went on to change its name from
Coopers to Jockey.

Who invented roller skates?

A guy called Joseph
Merlin showed off
his roller-skate
invention at a grand
ball in Europe.
Merlin entered the
ballroom gliding on
wheels and playing
a violin. It was
one trick too many
because Merlin lost
control and crashed into a huge
ballroom mirror.

The first postage stamp in England
was known as the Penny Black
because it was issued in 1840
when the public had a choice of
envelopes in two prices—a penny
black or a two penny blue.

Potato chips were invented after a guy eating in the Moon Lake House Hotel in Saratoga Springs, New York, complained that his fried potatoes were too thick. So, the chef hit back—sending out the thinnest, skinniest potato slices anyone had seen.

The chef's name has not lasted with the story. But historians tell us that potato chips made their first appearance in London, England in 1913.

What do BC and AD stand for?
These letters usually appear with dates, like 200 BC or AD 316. BC means before Christ was born, and AD means after the birth of Jesus (it stands for *Anno Domini,* which is Latin for "in the year of our Lord." Many people write "BCE," which stands for "Before Common Era" as not everybody believes in Christianity.

Why do we call a honeymoon a "honeymoon"?
It goes back to the days of Babylon, 4,000 years ago, when for a month after a wedding, the bride's father supplied his son-in-law with all the mead he could drink. Mead is a honey beer. This period was known as a "honey month."

How big is the Universe?
The most distant objects that astronomers can see are "quasars," which are up to 15 billion light years away. I don't know what quasars are though.

But I can tell you about the Big Bang. It's the name given to the explosion that astronomers think started the universe. It was massive. All the material in the universe was in the form of energy condensed into a tiny space. Starting from nothing, a second or two into the Big Bang the universe was smaller than a Ping-Pong ball.

At the time of the explosion the temperature was around 18,000 degrees Fahrenheit. As the temperature cooled atoms began to form. After a while these atoms began to clump together and the first galaxies were made. The outer galaxies of the universe are still moving away into space at great speed which shows that the universe is still expanding.

atoms clumping galaxies

(useless diagram)

What exactly is the "soul"?
I looked this one up. It's a bit like mist only finer. According to a Princeton University source, soul is "the immaterial part of a person ..." It's that crap feeling you get inside when you do something that you know is wrong.
So that's what we mean when we say something is "bad for the soul." But there's just as much stuff going on that is good for the soul. Like diving into the sea, or biting into a slab of chocolate.

"Soul food" is African American food-grits, bacon, stuff that is not all that good for your body but it feels right, and so, it goes by soul food.
"Soul music" is that feel good music (African American in origin). James Brown is The King of Soul.
"Soul Train" is one of the all-time big soul hits.
"Soul mate" is that person you feel specially connected to. You have the same beliefs and enjoy similar things.

Sole is a fish. The rest of the time it's the bottom of your foot.

sole
sole

Sports stuff

The ball is the single most important development in the history of sport.
Early Egyptians and Sumerians played with a ball shaped out of light wood or strips of leather stitched together and stuffed with hair, feathers, and cloth.

The earliest known rubber ball belonged to the Aztec Indians. Travelers as early as the 15th century described Aztecs "bouncing balls."

Bowling is one of the oldest known sports. Among the things found with an Egyptian child buried around 5200 BC were a number of vertical stone pins. A round stone was rolled to topple them.

Most people think that skiing is a modern sport but skis found in bogs in Sweden and Finland date between 4,000 and 5,000 years old. A rock carving of two men on skis found in a Norwegian cave has been dated back to 2000 BC.

An Egyptian copper statuette depicting wrestling is over 3,000 years old!

The Athens Olympics in 1896 has been described as the "first modern Olympics." But only 311 athletes took part and over 230 of these athletes came from Greece. The first gold medal went to an American, James B. Connolly, for winning the hop, skip, and jump.

Sleeping beauties

Why do we and most animals need to sleep?
Sleep gives our bodies the chance to repair muscles and replace dead cells.
Sleep also gives the brain a chance to file away stuff and sort out our memories.

Swifts and frigate birds do not drop
to earth to sleep. They sleep on
the wing.

Sometimes when you feel lousy it's
because you haven't had enough
sleep. If you miss two nights it
gets worse. You can't concentrate.
You make mistakes. After three
days of no sleep, you can't think
clearly.

zzz...humph? zzz

Do whales and dolphins sleep?
Nope, and sort of. Humans don't have to stop and think
about breathing–we just do it. Whales and dolphins are
different. They have to keep moving to breathe. So what
happens is they close down one half of the brain and
lounge for long periods. But they are never completely
asleep like us. They catnap in a dolphinish and whale–
like way.

My dad snores. Sometimes he's so noisy
my mom has to go and sleep on the couch.
Once he made a glass rattle on his
bedside table.
I don't snore. Nor does my mom. The
reason why my dad snores has to do
with the soft tissue at the back of his
throat. We all have it. It's the same
stuff that allows you to swallow and
gurgle.
With snoring, the problem is too much
tissue. The tissue relaxes and vibrates
against the back of the throat during
breathing and that's what you hear.
It's the same thing when your dog snores.
Budgies don't snore, nor do snakes,
insects, or snails. Fish don't either.
I'm not sure if elephants snore. If they
do I wouldn't like to sleep near one.
An elephant's trunk can weigh up to 396
pounds and measure 6.9 feet long. A trunk
has more than 40,000 muscles and tendons
and there are nerve ends at
the tip of the trunk. There
are also two small fingers
for picking up smaller
things. So an elephant's
trunk can pick up a log
or an ice block ...Or write a novel
or a stick.

Conversation stoppers

A normal breath travels at 4 miles per hour. A sneeze travels at 100 miles per hour.

Have you ever wondered where flies go for winter? Most of them die, leaving their eggs to see them through the winter. Cluster flies look for a warm nook or cranny of a house and maybe fly out on the odd warm winter's afternoon. Mosquitoes are like bears. *I die* ~ *they both bite!* They sleep all winter. Mosquitoes look for a damp hiding place such as a house basement. In spring the females become active-they fly around for food (that's us)! Once they've had their blood lunch they're ready to lay eggs. Male mosquitoes don't drink blood. They live on nectar and pollen.

What did New Zealand mosquitoes and sandflies eat before people provided them with blood? Seals, penguins, and other birds.

Stuff to wonder aloud on a long car trip

Why don't haircuts hurt? Because the only part of our hair that is alive is under the scalp; that's why it hurts when someone pulls our hair.

Why do we have eyebrows? They stop the rain or sweat running into our eyes. They also help us communicate in non-verbal ways. For example, the raised eyebrow can mean two things: "Hello I'm pleased to see you" and "You are a liar. You are full of crap."

How fast does your hair grow?

About .02 inches a day—or about 6 inches a year. Your hair on your head grows constantly where as the hair on your arms is programmed to stop after a few months. Otherwise we'd be shaggier than goats.

Things your younger brothers and sisters will ask

Where does rain come from?

Warm air turns the water from rivers, lakes, and the sea into water vapor that rises into the air. The water vapor forms clouds which contain small drops of water or ice crystals depending on how high the clouds are. This then drops to earth as rain or if it is cold enough it turns into snow.

approx 10m in a lifetime

If the rain drops pure water over oceans why is seawater salty?
Because the sun burns off the pure water. About 3.5 percent of seawater is salt.
Don't let your dog drink it, although dogs usually know.
Cats sometimes drink swimming pool water on hot days. So do bumblebees, which is why you find them floating around on top.
If humans drink seawater they become dehydrated.

More than 70 percent of the earth is covered in water.
60 percent of the human body is water.

Where did the Earth get its water? From millions of comets which hit the Earth about 4,600,000,000 years ago. Scientists say the comets were little more than big snowballs.

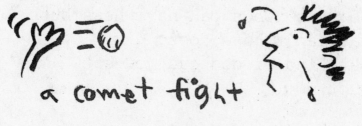

a comet fight

Global warming is the trend
that sees the earth's atmosphere
getting warmer. As a result,
the ice caps are
getting smaller,
the water levels
are rising. In
the future, small
islands in the
Pacific may sink
below the ocean.

Why do dogs chase their tails?

It may be because they have fleas
or an itch. Or they may be showing
off and looking for attention.
Scientists say it's best not to
laugh or make any comment when a dog
is chasing its tail.
What's the difference between dogs
and fleas? Dogs can have fleas but
fleas can't have dogs.
What kind of dog can you eat?
A hot dog.

Things we live with without thinking about why

Have you noticed how the days of the week are named after planets? The names of the days of the week are also some of the oldest words in English. For example, Sunday is named after "Sun's Day." In Anglo-Saxon it is Sunnan Daeg. Monday is Monan Daeg, "Moon's Day."

Tuesday (Mars Day) in Anglo-Saxon is "Tiwes Daeg." Tir is an Anglo-Saxon spelling of Tyr, the Norse God of War.

Wednesday (Mercury's Day) in Anglo-Saxon is "Wodens Daeg."

Thursday (Jupiter's Day), or Thor's Day, the Norse God of Thunder, is "Thurs Daeg" in Anglo-Saxon.

Friday (Day of Venus) is "Frige Daeg" in Anglo-Saxon after Frigga, the Norse God of Love.

Saturday (Saturn's Day) is "Satern Daeg" in Anglo-Saxon.

What makes a cake rise in the oven?
Cakes contain an ingredient called
yeast. When heated it reproduces
itself to double, triple, or even
quadruple its size.

Why do we blow out candles on our
birthdays?
In many cultures fire represents light so blowing out
a candle could symbolize the closing of a year and
the celebration of the year to come.

*because if we didn't,
the cake would
catch fire!*

Ever wondered why we shiver?
If you get too cold, muscles all
over your body quickly tighten and
loosen. This is called shivering.
Scientists say "shivering" is what
warms us up even though most of the
time we're shivering we're actually
freezing our butts off.

Why does ice cream melt?
It returns to liquid form when heat breaks apart
the molecules which stick together when cold. The
hotter the day is, the faster it melts.

What is cotton candy made of?
Melted sugar spun in a machine to
form threads of sugar.

Who invented tree
forts?
The point of a tree fort used to be
to get a safe distance away from
dangerous animals on the ground.

Where does all the garbage go?
Some of it is taken to the dump which
is sometimes called a landfill. It just
decomposes into the ground. Some garbage
is burned or washed into the sea although
this is bad for the environment.

When you take a pee where does it go?
Well, supposing you have just gone to
the toilet the pee travels down a waste
pipe and joins all the pee coming from
other houses. What was a trickle soon
becomes a flood. The pee travels to a
treatment plant where in some countries
it is purified and returns to your house
via the kitchen tap. So, you get to drink
what you peed out minus the wastes. In
London, they say that a cup of water is
recycled in this way an average of six
times. So Londoners when they fill up a
glass with water are drinking what other
people peed out a few weeks ago. This
is one of the reasons why water tastes
differently from one place to another.

Why do leaves fall off the trees in
autumn?
On some trees they don't–that's why these trees are
called "evergreens." On other trees, which are known as
"deciduous," as temperatures decrease and leaves have
finished growing, they grow old and weak, and their stems
grow frail and break off. This gives a chance for new buds
to grow when spring comes around.

Why don't tattoos rub off?

They are a permanent stain like spilled juice on a creamy carpet. A pigment dissolves into ruptures of your skin. People wear tats for different reasons. A girl might want to remember her boyfriend's name WAYNE. But will she want to remember him forever? That's a question worth asking before you decide on getting a tat. Remember it's a lifelong thing. These days you can get them surgically removed but they still leave a scar. In some cultures, tats were worn to ward away evil spirits or they indicated rank and status such as the moko among Maori.

"To the end of the Earth" is a weird expression because no such place actually exists. The Earth is round so one line joins up to become a circle where there is no beginning and no edge. You might as well look for an edge on a round stone.

But if the Earth is round how come we don't fall off?

Earth is so huge that the curve is very gradual-we don't even notice this and therefore it feels like it's flat. Plus, gravity holds us in place. Gravity is what sits behind the saying-"What goes up must come down."

Do pirates still exist?

They were famous around the Caribbean. Pirates still operate in the seas of east Asia where boats and ships have been known to go missing. But today when people speak of piracy it usually means they have been ripped off, as in the pizza joint which charges too much for extras, "they're a bunch of pirates."

What happens to puddles after it stops raining?

The sun evaporates the puddle into steam that rises into the atmosphere and then turns into cloud (see rain on page 154).

Why do flowers smell sweet?

Flowers give off a scent to attract bees, butterflies, and moths to come and pollinate them.

The largest flower in the world is called a *Rafflesia* and it grows in Asia to 36 inches across. Its name means "stinking corpse flower." But the bees must like them.

Where do marbles come from?

Around 3000 BC the Romans used to play a game called "nuts," and the game grew then on. It wasn't until 1846 that a German glassblower invented some special scissors which turned out to be a useful tool for making marbles.

How come glass is see-through?
Because it is actually made of
melted sand that when turned into
liquid becomes see-through and
when dried remains that way.

Ice-skating is
one of the oldest
sports in the world.
Around 1000 BC they
were ice-skating in
Scandinavia where
they used bone or
the rib of the elk
for ice-skating
blades. Bone was
used for ice-skating in England up
until the 12th century.

Why do cartoon characters always wear the same
clothes? It's so we will recognize who they are. Clothes
are one clue. If you were to look in the wardrobe of a
cartoon character you would find racks of exactly the
same clothes so don't worry about their hygiene.

what did you do today?

breathed

In the course of our lifetime what thing do we do the most of? Going to the toilet, eating, playing, sleeping? None of those, dummies. Think about it. We breathe. People average 20 breaths a minute, that's around 10 million breaths a year.

Airplanes are huge and heavy so why don't they fall out of the sky? A lot of the reason is the shape of the wings. The faster the plane goes, the less air that is on top of the wings—most of it is underneath which supports the plane. The tail balances the flight.

What was the first TV program ever? *The Queen's Messenger* was a drama broadcast in 1928. The first TV cartoon was *Fantasmagorie* by Emile Reynaud of France. The first cartoon with sound was Walt Disney's *Steamboat Willie* in 1928, which was an early version of Mickey Mouse.

Who invented envelopes?

Well, clay wrappers were used by the
Babylonians to protect documents from
prying eyes as far back as 2000 BC.
Henry VIII of England appointed a
master of posts who delivered all the
king's documents. In the 16th century
official letters were sent "under cover
or envelope."

Why do the stars twinkle?

There are over 6,000 stars that are
visible from every point on Earth.
It takes a while for the star's
light to become visible to us-
years in fact. The light has to
travel through the atmosphere before
reaching our eyes and it is not a
straight path. The light is wavy so
it appears to be twinkling.

How does the sun know when to rise? It's not the sun's idea when to rise or not-the sun is as stationary as a streetlight. It's the earth that moves, and as it rotates it gives the appearance of the sun moving across the sky from dawn to dusk.

Where does the wind come from?

In ancient Greek mythology the god Aeolus kept the winds in a cave and unleashed them to create a storm. But in everyday life it is the sun that creates wind. When air gets hot it rises so other air rushes in to take its place. This movement causes different wind patterns.

wind diagram:

Why is the sea salty?
It's mainly salt rubbed off rocks.
The smart aleck answer is that
God looked at the instructions
which said "just add water."

Has a kid ever ruled a country?
Yep. King Tutankhamen was an
Egyptian pharaoh. He died when
he was about 18 years old
c. 1352 BC. He ruled for nine
years and is often called the
Boy King.

When did a meteorite last hit Earth?
About 20,000 meteorites hit earth
every year. In 1992, a small
meteorite landed on a car in New
York. In 2004, a small meteorite
crashed into the lounge of a house
in Auckland, New Zealand.

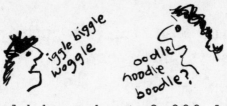

The world has about 8,000 languages
but one dies out nearly every day.
More people speak Mandarin Chinese
than any other language. Then come
English, the languages of India,
Spanish, and Arabic. The English
language is changing so quickly
that next century people will have
difficulty making sense of it.

Crazy People stuff

What are the craziest things
people do? Depends on what you
call crazy. If it's sticking 151
drinking straws in your mouth then
American Jim Purol is your man.
If it is growing your fingernails
to 20.18 feet then the Indian guy
Shridhar Chillal is the craziest.
I think the things we do for fun
like jumping out of airplanes with

a parachute and bungee jumping are pretty crazy but good fun at the same time. There's a lot of things that fall into that category. Or maybe it's those TV reality shows like *Big Brother*. Or maybe it's people who smoke and eats loads of junk food and who know it's bad for them who could be called crazy.

Kevin Cole of New Mexico holds the world record for blowing a strand of spaghetti out his nostril. He achieved this record on December 16, 1998, blowing a strand of spaghetti out his nostril for a distance of 7.5 inches. Gross fact: He didn't just stuff the spaghetti up his nose. Kevin actually swallowed the spaghetti and used his tongue to shift it up his nostril.

Another guy, Garry Turner from the UK, managed to clip 153 wooden clothes pegs to his face at the offices of the Guinness Book of Records on August 3, 2002.

Here are some crazy things people have done
for religious reasons:

1. A man in India kept his hand in the air
   for about 30 years as a sign of his
   devotion to the Hindu God, Shiva.

2. Another man from India rolled 2,485
   miles to pay homage to the goddess
   Vaishno Devi. He only stopped for water
   and cigarettes.

3. A man from America once walked 33,150
   miles carrying a big wooden cross.

Some Interesting Stuff about Colors:

Yellow–this is the first color seen by babies,
although when they are first born they can only see
black and white.

Lemon Yellow is the most tiring color to look at for a
long time.

Green is the most restful color
and most people hate wearing it.

Blue is the one adults like the best. Kids get better marks when they have tests in rooms with blue ceilings. Blue is also the worst color for food to be.

Pink is the most calming color, which is why a center for violent kids in California has pink walls. Purple is the hardest color to see.
Red is the one kids like best. Scientists say red is energizing, aggressive, and exciting. Brazil and Ecuador used to have a lot of accidents involving red cars so now red cars are illegal in those countries.

Fancy LINES to use on girls:

"Haven't I seen you before? Oh yeah, it was in my dreams."

"My love is like a red, red rose." (Robert Burns)

"How do I love thee, let me count the ways . . ." (Elizabeth Barrett Browning)

a line I think would work:
"If I tell you you're beautiful, what will you do for me?"

Topics of conversation

Safe topics with parents include: school, sport, weather
With grandparents: *The Sound of Music*, those were the days, food
With friends: movies, clothes, concerts, parties, and associated upcoming events

don't get it wrong!

What not to bring up with friends: *The Sound of Music*, weather, those were the days
What not to bring up with grandparents: concerts, parties
What not to bring up with parents: money, parties, and associated upcoming events

Some dos and don'ts on the kissing biz–
Don't do the "washing machine"
thing with your tongue.
Remember—the mouth is the
target. Brush your teeth. Suck
a peppermint or a boiled sweet.
Chances are the kisser will
recognize the flavor because
the tongue has between 3,000 and
10,000 taste buds.

Remember: don't
slobber. Your mouth
produces about a
quart of saliva a
day. Don't kiss a
cow because cows
make 200 times more
saliva than humans.
Remember-to breathe. Humans need at
least 20 breaths a minute.
Don't panic-the thrashing around in
your chest is your heart beating
stronger.

Puberty-the big questions:

What makes boys' voices go
squeaky? Your voice box grows
bigger, sometimes quite rapidly.
Relax, it doesn't go on forever.
After a while it settles down and
one morning you wake up and find
your voice has gone deeper.

Why are you so much smaller than your mates?
Because puberty takes place at
a different point for every
person; anywhere between 8 and
17 for girls, and 10 and 18 for
guys.

You've heard about trees and stuff experiencing "growth spurts" in spring– well, we humans experience the same. A growth spurt happens in puberty. All the body parts don't necessarily grow at the same rate. First, your feet and hands get bigger, then arms and legs lengthen, then about a year later the rest of your body catches up.

Ever wondered what breasts are made of?

During puberty fat forms in the breasts to cushion the milk producing ducts. Some girls worry about the size of their breasts but their main purpose is to produce milk and size doesn't matter. All sizes can feed babies.

Neck-row-tie-zing-fash-ee-eye-tis
otherwise known as necrotizing
fasciitis is a rare flesh-eating
disease where death can occur in
12-24 hours. You can relax. It's a
lot more rare than say zits.

Why do we get zits (pimples)?

The oil glands in our skin are
affected by hormonal change,
a kind of chemical reaction,
making the skin
oily. Good diet,
lots of water,
keeping your
skin clean-all
this helps keep
the dreaded zits
at bay.

a swarm
of zits

Cool things about growing up

1. You get stronger. At birth 20 percent of the body is muscle, 25 percent in early puberty, 45 percent as a young adult.

2. You get to stay out later

3. You learn to drive

4. Make your own decisions

5. More parties and privileges

6. Get into R-rated movies

Once upon a time, people used to
sit around and talk, read and
play cards, gather around the
piano. That all changed with
the invention of the TV in 1927.
Today, some 500 million homes
worldwide have TV sets. We may not
live next door to
every human on the
planet, but we can
see into the way
other people live
through TV. This
is what is meant
by the "global
village." We are
all hooked up
electronically.
Same thing goes with texting, the
phone, and the Internet. This is
a different kind of web to the
one that I started the book with.
Ducks have webbed feet. Some books
create a web of intrigue. You can
create your own web. Be curious
and follow your nose. You will
be surprised at where it leads

WWD
(world wide
duck)

and all the stuff you find out.
After you have collected your
information: join the dots. And
hey presto! You've created your
own web.

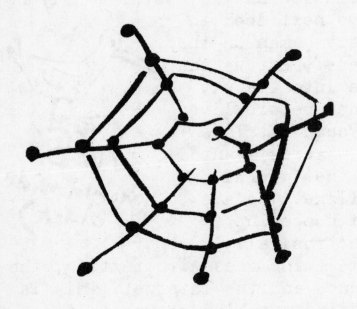

For a Simon Eliot screensaver
and other surprises go to
www.simoneliot.com